Marcus Dods

How to become like Christ and other papers

Marcus Dods

How to become like Christ and other papers

ISBN/EAN: 9783741132339

Manufactured in Europe, USA, Canada, Australia, Japa

Cover: Foto ©Andreas Hilbeck / pixelio.de

Manufactured and distributed by brebook publishing software (www.brebook.com)

Marcus Dods

How to become like Christ and other papers

HOW TO BECOME LIKE CHRIST,

And Other Papers.

By Marcus Dods, D.D.

NEW YORK: THOS. WHITTAKER,
2 & 3, Bible House.   1897.

Contents.

	PAGE
How to Become Like Christ	1
The Transfiguration	37
Indiscreet Importunity	67
Shame on Account of God's Displeasure	83
Naaman Cured	101
The Lame Man at the Temple Gate	119

How to Become Like Christ.

HOW TO BECOME LIKE CHRIST.

"But we all, with unveiled face reflecting as a mirror the glory of the Lord, are changed into the same image from glory to glory, even as by the Spirit of the Lord."—2 Cor. iii. 18 (Revised Version).

I SUPPOSE there is almost no one who would deny, if it were put to him, that the greatest possible attainment a man can make in this world is likeness to the Lord Jesus Christ. Certainly no one would deny that there is nothing but character that we can carry out of life with us, and that our prospect of good in any future life will certainly vary with the resemblance of our character to that of Jesus Christ, which is to rule the whole future. We all admit that; but almost every one of us offers to himself some apology for not being like Christ, and has scarcely any clear reality of aim of becoming like Him. Why, we say to ourselves, or we say in our practice, it is really impossible in a world such as ours is to become perfectly holy. One or two men in a century may become great saints; given a certain natural disposition and given exceptionally favouring circumstances, men may become saintly; but surely the ordinary run of men, men such as we know ourselves to be, with secular disposition and with many strong, vigorous passions—surely we can really not be expected to become like Christ, or, if it is expected of us, we know that it is impossible. On the contrary, Paul says, "We all," "We all." Every Christian has that for a destiny: to be changed into the image of his Lord. And he not only says so, but in this one verse he reveals to us the mode of becoming like Christ, and a mode, as we shall find, so simple and so infallible in its working that a man cannot understand it without renewing his hope that even he may one day become like Christ.

In order to understand this simplest mode of sanctification we must look back at the incident that we read in the Book of Exodus (xxxiv. 29-35.). Paul had been reading how when Moses came down from the mount where he had been speaking with God his face shone, so as to dazzle and alarm those who were near him. They at once recognised that that was the glory of God reflected from him; and just as it is almost as difficult for us to look at the sun reflected from a mirror as to look directly at the sun, so these men felt it almost as difficult to look straight at the face of Moses as to look straight at the face of God. But Moses was a wise man, and he showed his wisdom in this instance as well as elsewhere. He knew that that glory was only on the skin of his face, and that of course it would pass away. It was a superficial shining. And accordingly he put a veil over his face, that the children of Israel might not see it dying out from minute to minute and from hour to hour, because he knew these Israelites thoroughly, and he knew that when they saw the glory dying out they would say, "God has forsaken Moses. We need not attend to him any more. His authority is gone, and the glory of God's presence has passed from him." So Moses wore the veil that they might not see the glory dying out. But whenever he was called back to the presence of God he took off the veil and received a new access of glory on his face, and thus went "from glory to glory."

"That," says Paul, "is precisely the process through which we Christian men become like Christ." We go back to the presence of Christ with unveiled face; and as often as we stand in His presence, as often as we deal in our spirit with the living Christ, so often do we take on a little of His glory. The glory of Christ is His character; and as often as we stand before Christ, and think of Him, and realise what He was, our heart goes out and reflects some of His character. And that reflection, that glory, is not any longer merely on the skin of the face; as Paul wishes us to recognise, it is a spiritual glory, it is wrought by the

Spirit of Christ upon our spirit, and it is we ourselves that are changed from glory to glory into the very image of the Lord.

Now obviously this mode of sanctification has extraordinary recommendations. In the first place, it is absolutely simple. If you go to some priest or spiritual director, or minister of the Gospel, or friend, and ask what you are to do if you wish to become a holy man, why, even the best of them will almost certainly tell you to read certain books, to spend so much time in prayer and reading your Bible, to go regularly to church, to engage in this and that good work. If you had applied to a spiritual director of the middle ages of this world's history and of the history of Christianity, he would have told you that you must retire from the world altogether in order to become holy. Paul says, "Away with all that nonsense!" We are living in a real world; Christ lived in a real world: Christ did not retire from men. And He says all that you have to do in order to be like Christ is to carry His image with you in your heart. That is all. To be with Him, to let Him stand before you and command your love, that will infallibly change you into His image. I do not know that we sufficiently recognise the simplicity of Christian methods. We do not understand what Paul meant by proclaiming it as the religion of the spirit, as a religion superior to everything mechanical and external. Think of the deliverance it was for him who had grown up under a religion which commanded him to go a long journey three times a year, to take the best of his goods and offer them in the Temple, to comply with a multitude of oppressive observances and ordinances. Think of the emancipation when he found a spiritual religion. Why, in those times a man must have despaired of becoming a holy man; but now Paul says you will infallibly become holy if you learn this easy lesson of carrying the Lord Jesus with you in your heart.

Another recommendation of this method is that it is so obviously grounded on our own nature. No sooner are we told by Paul that we must act as mirrors of Christ than we recognise that nature has made us to be mirrors, that we cannot but reflect what is passing before us. You are walking along the street, and a little child runs before a carriage; you shrink back as if you were in danger. You see a man fall from a scaffolding, crushed; your face takes on an expression of pain, reflecting what is passing in him. You go and spend an evening with a man much stronger, much purer, much saner, than yourself, and you come away knowing yourself a stronger and a better man. Why? Because you are a mirror, because in your inmost nature you have responded to and reflected the good that was in him. Look into any family, and what do you see? You see the boy, not imitating consciously, but taking on, his father's looks and attitudes and ways; and as the boy grows up these become his own looks and attitudes and ways. He has reflected his father from one degree of proficiency unto another, from one intimacy, from one day's observation of his father to another, until he is the image of the old man over again.

"Similarly," says Paul, "live with Christ; learn to carry His image with you, learn to adore Him, learn to love Him, and infallibly, whether you will or not, by this simple method you will become Christ over again; you will become conformed, as God means you to become conformed, to the image of His Son."

This has been tested by the experience of thousands; and it has been found to be a true method. Every one who spends but two minutes in the morning in the observation of Christ, every one who will be at the pains to let the image of Christ rise before him and to remember the purity, the unworldliness, the heavenliness, the godliness of Jesus Christ, that man is the better for this exercise. And how utterly useless is it to offer any other method of sanctification to thousands of our fellow-citizens. How can many of our fellow-citizens secrete themselves for prayer? If you ask them to go and pray as you pray in your comfortable home, if you ask them to read the Bible before they go out at five or six o'clock in the morning, do you expect that your word will be followed? Why, the thing is impossible. But ask a man to carry Christ with him in his mind, that is a thing he can do; and if he does it once, if only once the man sees Christ before him, realises that this living Person is with him, and remembers the character of Christ as it is written for us in the Gospels, that man knows that he has made a step in advance, knows that he is the better for it, knows that he does reflect for a little, even though it be but for a little, the very image of the Lord Jesus Christ; and other people know it also.

Now, if that is so, there are obviously three things that we must do. <u>We must, in the first place, learn to associate with</u> Christ. I say that even one reflection does something, but we need to reflect Christ constantly, continually, if we are to become like Him. When you pass away from before a mirror the reflection also goes. In the case of Moses the reflection stayed for a little, and that is perhaps a truer figure of what happens to the Christian who sets Christ before him and reflects Him. But very often as soon as Christ is not consciously remembered you fall back to other remembrances and reflect other things. You go out in the morning with your associates, and they carry you away; you have not as yet sufficiently impressed upon yourself the image of Christ. Therefore we must learn to carry Christ with us always, as a constant Companion. Some one may say that is impossible. No one will say it is impossible who is living in absence from any one he loves. What happens when we are living separated from some one we love? This happens: that his image is continually in our minds. At the most unexpected times that image rises, and especially if we are proposing to ourselves to do what that person would not approve. At once his image rises to rebuke us and to hold us back. So that it is not only possible to carry with us the image of Christ: it is absolutely certain that we shall carry that image with us, if only we give Him that love and reverence which is due from every human being. Who has done for us what Christ has done? Who commands our reverence as He does? If once He gets hold of our affection, it is impossible that He should not live constantly in our hearts. And if we say that persons deeply immersed in business cannot carry Christ with them thus, remember what He Himself says: "If any man love Me, he will keep My word; and My Father will love him, and we will come unto him." So that He is most present with the busiest and with those who strive as best they can to keep His commandments.

But we must not only associate with Christ and make Him our constant company: we must, in the second place, set ourselves square with Christ. You know that if you look into a mirror obliquely, if a mirror is not set square with you, you do not see yourself, but what is at the opposite angle, something that is pleasant or something that is disagreeable to you; it matters not—you cannot see yourself. And unless we as mirrors set ourselves perfectly square with Christ, we do not reflect Him, but perhaps things that are in His sight monstrous. And, in point of fact, that is what happens with most of us, because it is here that we are chiefly tried. All persons brought up within the Christian Church pay some attention to Christ. We too well understand His excellence and we too well understand the advantages of being Christian men not to pay some attention to Christ. But that will not make us conform to His image. In order to be conformed to the image of Christ we must be wholly His. Suppose you enter a studio where a sculptor is working, will he hand you his hammer and chisel to finish the most difficult piece of his work or to do any part of it? Assuredly not. It is his own idea that he is working out, and none but his own hand can work it out. So with us who are to be moulded by Christ. Christ cannot mould us into His image unless we are wholly His. Every stroke that is made upon us by the chisel and mallet of the world is lost to His ideal. As often as we reflect what is not purely Christian, so often do we mar the image of Christ.

Now how is it with us? Need we ask? When we go along the street, what is it that we reflect? Do we not reflect a thousand things that Christ disapproves? What is it that our heart responds to when we are engaged in business? Is it to appeals that this world makes to us? Is it the appeal that a prospect of gain makes to us that we respond to eagerly? That is what is making us; that is what is moulding and making us the men that we are destined to be. We are moulded into the character that we are destined to live with for ever and ever, by our likings and dislikings, by the actual response that we are now giving day by day to the things that we have to do with in this world. We may loathe the character of the sensualist; no language is too strong for us when we speak of him: but if we, in point of fact, respond to appeals made to the flesh rather than appeals made to the spirit, we are becoming sensual. We may loathe and despise the character of the avaricious worldly man; we may see its littleness, and pettiness, and greed, and selfishness: but do our own hearts go out in response to any offer of gain more eagerly than they go out to Christian work or to the interests of Christ's kingdom? Then we are becoming worldly and avaricious; we are becoming the very kind of men that we despise.

Of course we know this. We know that we are being made by what we respond to, and the older we grow we know it the more clearly; we see it written on our own character that we have become the kind of men that we little thought one day we should become, and we know that we have become such men by responding to certain things which are not the things of the Spirit. Never was a truer word said than that he that soweth to the flesh shall of the flesh reap corruption, and he only that soweth to the Spirit shall reap life. That is what in other terms Paul here says. He says, "If you set yourselves square with Christ, you will become like Him; that is to say, if you find your all in Him, if you can be absolutely frank and honest with Him, if you can say, 'Mould and fashion me according to Thy will; lead me according to Thy will; make me in this world what Thou wilt; do with me what Thou wilt: I put myself wholly at Thy disposal; I do not wish to crane to see past Christ's figure to some better thing beyond; I give myself wholly and freely to Him'—the man that says this, the man that does this, he will certainly become like to Him. But the man who even when he prays knows that he has desires in his heart that Christ cannot gratify, the man that never goes out from his own home or never goes into his own home without knowing that he has responded to things that Christ disapproves— how can that man hope to be like Him?"

We must then associate with Christ, and we must set ourselves squarely; we must be absolutely true in our entire and absolute devotion. Surely no man thinks that this is a hardship; that his nature and life will be restricted by giving himself wholly to Christ? It is only, as every Christian will tell you—it is only when you give yourself entirely to Christ that you know what freedom means; that you know what it is to live in this world afraid of nothing. Superior to things that before you were afraid of and anxious about, you at length learn what it is to be a child of God. Let no man think that he lames his nature and makes his life poorer by becoming entirely the possession of Christ.

But, thirdly, we must set Christ before us and live before Him with unveiled face. "We all *with unveiled face* reflecting as a mirror." Throw a napkin over a mirror, and it reflects nothing. Perfect beauty may stand before it, but the mirror gives no sign. And this is why in a dispensation like ours, the Christian dispensation, with everything contrived to reflect Christ, to exhibit Christ, the whole thing set a-going for this purpose of exhibiting Christ, we so little see Him. How is it that two men can sit at a Communion table together, and the one be lifted to the seventh heaven and see the King in His beauty, while the other only envies his neighbour his vision? Why is it that in the same household two persons will pass through identically the same domestic circumstances, the same events, from year to year, and the one see Christ everywhere, while the other grows sullen, sour, indifferent? Why is it? Because the one wears a veil that prevents him from seeing Christ; the other lives with unveiled face. How was it that the Psalmist, in the changes of the seasons even, in the mountain, in the sea, in everything that he had to do, found God? How was it that he knew that even though he made his bed in hell he would find God? Because he had an unveiled face; he was prepared to find God. How is it that many of us can come into church and be much more taken up with the presence of some

friend than with the presence of
Christ? The same reason still:
we wear a veil; we do not come
with unveiled face prepared to see
Him.

And when we ask ourselves,
"What, in point of fact, is the
veil that I wear? What is it that
has kept me from responding to
the perfect beauty of Christ's
character? I know that that
character is perfect; I know that
I ought to respond to it; I know
that I ought to go out eagerly
towards Christ and strive to
become like Him; why do I not
do it?" we find that the veil that
keeps us from responding thus to
Christ and reflecting Him is not
like the mere dimness on a mirror
which the bright and warm presence of Christ Himself would dry
off; it is like an incrustation that
has been growing out from our

hearts all our life long, and that now is impervious, so far as we can see, to the image of Christ. How can hearts steeped in worldliness reflect this absolutely unworldly, this heavenly Person? When we look into our hearts, what do we find in point of fact? We find a thousand things that we know have no right there; that we know to be wrong. How can such hearts reflect this perfect purity of Christ? Well, we must see to it that these hearts be cleansed; we must hold ourselves before Christ until from very shame these passions of ours are subdued, until His purity works its way into our hearts through all obstructions; and we must keep our hearts, we must keep the mirror free from dust, free from incrustations, once we have cleansed it.

LIKE CHRIST. 27

In some circumstances you might be tempted to say that really it is not so much that there is a veil on the mirror as that there is no quicksilver at all behind. You meet in life characters so thin, so shallow, that every good thought seems to go through and out of them at the other side; they hear with one ear, and it goes out at the other. You can make no impression upon them. There is nothing to impress, no character there to work upon. They are utterly indifferent to spiritual things, and never give a thought to their own character. What is to be done with such persons? God is the great Teacher of us all; God, in His providence, has made many a man who has begun life as shallow and superficial as man can be, deep enough before He has done with him.

Two particulars in which the perfectness of this method appears may be pointed out. First of all, it is perfect in this: that any one who begins it is bound to go on to the end. The very nature of the case leads him to go on and on from glory to glory, back and back to Christ, until the process is actually completed, and he is like Christ. The reason is this: that the Christian conscience is never much taken up with attainment made, but always with attainment that is yet to be made. It is the difference not the likeness that touches the conscience. A friend has been away in Australia for ten years, and he sends you his likeness, and you take it out eagerly, and you say, "Yes, the eyes are the very eyes; the brow, the hair are exactly like," but there is something about the mouth that you do not like, and you thrust it away in a drawer and never look at it again. Why? Because the one point of unlikeness destroys the whole to you. Just so when any Christian presents himself before Christ it is not the points of likeness, supposing there are any, which strike his conscience—it is the remaining points of difference that inevitably strike him, and so he is urged on and on from one degree of proficiency to another until the process is completed, because there is no point at which a man has made a sufficient attainment in the likeness of Christ. There is no point at which Christ draws a line and says, "You will do well if you reach this height, and you need not strive further." Why, we should be dissatisfied, we should throw up our allegiance to Christ, if He treated us so. He is our ideal, and it is resemblance to Him that draws us and makes us strive forward; and so a man is bound to go on, and on, and on, still drawn on to his ideal, still rebuked by his shortcomings, until he perfectly resembles Christ.

And this character of Christ that is our ideal is not assumed by Him for the nonce. He did not change His nature when He came to this earth; He did not put on this character to set us an example. The things that He did, He did because it was His nature to do them. He came to this world because His love would not let Him stay away from us. It was His nature that brought Him here, and it is His nature to be what He is, and so His character is to become our nature; it is to be so wrought in us that we cannot give it up. It is our eternal character, and therefore any amount of pains is worth spending on the achievement of it.

The second point of perfectness lies here. You know that in painting a likeness or cutting out a bust one feature often may be almost finished while the rest are scarcely touched, but in standing before a mirror the whole comes out at once. Now we often in the Christian life deal with ourselves as if we were painters and sculptors, not as if we were mirrors; we hammer and chisel away at ourselves to bring out some resemblance to Christ in some particulars, thinking that we can do it piecemeal. We might as well try to feed up our body piecemeal; we might as well try to make our eye bright without giving our cheek colour and our hands strength. The body is a whole, and we must feed the whole and nourish the whole if any one part of it is to be vigorous.

So it is with character. The character is a whole, and you can only deal with your character as a whole. What has resulted when we have tried the other process? Sometimes we set ourselves to subdue a sin or cultivate a grace. Well, candidly say what has come of this. Judging from my own experience, I would say that this comes of it: that in three or four days you forget what sin it was that you were trying to subdue. The temptation is away, and the sin is not there, and you forget all about it. That is the very snare of sin. Or you become a little better in a point that you were trying to cultivate. In that grace you are a shade improved. But that only brings out more astoundingly your frightful shortcoming in other particulars. Now, adopting Paul's method, this happens: Christ acts on our character just as a person acts upon a mirror. The whole image is reflected at once. How is it that society moulds a man? How can you tell in what class in society a man has been brought up? Not by one thing, not by his accent, not by his bearing, not by his conduct, but by the whole man. And why? Because a man does not consciously imitate this or that feature of the society in which he is brought up, does not do it consciously at all; he is merely reflecting it as a mirror, and society acts on him as a whole, and makes him the man he is. "Just so," says Paul. "Live with Christ, and He will make you the man that you are destined to be."

One word in conclusion. I suppose there is no one who at one time or other has not earnestly desired to be of some use in the world. Perhaps there are few who have not even definitely desired to be of some use in the kingdom of Christ. As soon as we recognise the uniqueness of Christ's purpose and the uniqueness of His power in the world, as soon as we recognise that all good influence and all superlatively dominant influence proceeds from Him, and that really the hope of our race lies in Jesus Christ—as soon as we realise that, as soon as we see that with our reason, and not as a thing that we have been taught to believe, as soon as we lay hold on it for ourselves, we cannot but wish to do something to forward His purposes in the world. But as soon as we form the wish we say, "What can we do? We have not been born with great gifts; we have not been born in superior positions; we have not wealth; we are shut off from the common ways of doing good; we cannot teach in the Sabbath-school; we cannot go and preach; we cannot go and speak to the sick; we cannot speak even to our fellow at the desk. What can we do?" We can do the best thing of all, as of course all the best things are open to every man. Love, faith, joy, hope, all these things, all the best things, are open to all men; and so here it is open to all of us to forward the cause of Christ in the most influential way possible, if not in the most prominent way. What <u>happens when a person is looking into a shop window where there</u>

is a mirror, and some one comes up behind—some one he knows? He does not look any longer at the image; he turns to look at the person whose image is reflected. Or if he sees reflected on the mirror something very striking: he does not content himself with looking at the image; he turns and looks at the thing itself. So it is always with the persons that you have to do with. If you become a mirror to Christ your friends will detect it in a very few days; they will see appearing in you, the mirror, an image which they know has not been originated in you, and they will turn to look straight at the Person that you are reflecting. It is in that way that Christianity passes from man to man.

The Transfiguration.

THE TRANSFIGURATION.

> "And it came to pass about eight days after these sayings, He took Peter and John and James and went up into the mountain to pray."—LUKE ix. 28—36.

THE public life of our Lord falls into two parts; and the incident here recorded is the turning point between them. In order that He might leave behind Him when He died a sure foundation for His Church, it was necessary that His intimate companions should at all events know that He was the Christ, and that the Christ must enter into glory by suffering death. Only then, when they understood this, could He die and leave them on earth behind. Now it is just at this point in His life that it has become quite clear that the first article of the Christian creed—that Jesus is the Christ—had been at last definitely accepted by the disciples. Very solemnly our Lord has put it to them: "Who say ye that I am?" No doubt it was a trying moment for Him as for them. What was He to do if it had not now become plain at least to a few steadfast souls that He was the Christ—the Messenger of God to men? Happily the impulsiveness of Peter gives Him little space for anxiety; for he, with that generous outburst of affectionate trust which should ring through every creed, said, "Thou art the Christ, the Son of the living God." You see the intensified relief which this brought to our Lord, the keen satisfaction He felt as He heard it distinctly and solemnly uttered as the creed of the Twelve; as He heard what hitherto He

could only have gathered from
casual expressions, from wistful,
awe-struck looks, from overheard
questionings and debatings with
one another. You see how at once
He steps on to a new footing with
them, as He cordially, and with
intense gratitude, says to Peter,
"Blessed art thou, Simon Bar-
jona." In this Divinely-wrought
confession of Peter's, He finds at
last the foundation stone of the
earthly building, the beginning of
that intelligent and hearty recep-
tion of Himself which was to make
earth the recipient of all heaven's
fulness. But as yet only half the
work is done. Men believe that
He is the King, but as yet they
have very little idea of what the
kingdom is to consist. They think
Him worthy of all glory, but the
kind of glory, and the way to it,
they are ignorant of. From that

time forth, therefore, began Jesus to show unto them how He must go unto Jerusalem and suffer many things, even of the men who ought chiefly to have recognised Him, and to be raised again the third day.

Once before our Lord had been tempted in another way to the throne of the universal dominion of men; again this temptation is pressed upon Him by the very men who should have helped Him to resist it; His closest, His warmest, His most enlightened friends, those who stand on quite a different plane from the world at large, are His tempters. Satan found in them an adequate mouthpiece. They, who should have cheered and heartened Him to face the terrible prospect, were hindrances, were an additional burden and anxiety to Him.

Now, it is to this conversation that the incident known as the transfiguration is linked by all the evangelists who relate it—the first three. It was six days after (or, as Luke says, eight days after) this conversation that Jesus went up Mount Hermon for the sake of retirement and prayer. Plainly He was aware that the great crisis of His life had come. The time had come when He must cease teaching, and face His destiny. He had made upon His disciples an impression which would be indelible. With deliberation they had accepted Him as the Messiah; the Church was founded; His work, so far as His teaching went, was accomplished. It remained that He should die. To consecrate Himself to this hard necessity, He retired to the solitude of Mount Hermon. We start, then, from the wrong point of view, if we suppose that Jesus climbed Hermon in order to enjoy spiritual ecstasy, or exhibit His glory to those three men. Ecstasy of this kind must come unsought, and the way to it lies through conflict, humiliation, self-mastery. It was not simply to pray that Jesus retired; it was to engage in the great conflict of His life. And because He felt Himself so much in need of kindness and support, He took with Him the three companions He could most depend upon. They were loyal friends; and their very presence was a strength to Him. So human was Jesus, and now so heavily burdened, that the devotedness of these three plain men—the sound of their voices, the touch of their hands as they clambered the hill together, gave Him strength and courage. Let no one be ashamed to lean upon the affection of his fellow-men. Let us, also, reverently, and with sympathy, accompany our Lord and witness, and endeavour to understand, the conflict in which He now engaged.

It has been suggested that the transfiguration may best be understood as a temptation. Undoubtedly there must have been temptation in the experience of Jesus at this crisis. It was for the purpose of finally consecrating Himself to death, with all its painful accompaniments, that He now retired. But the very difficulty of this act of consecration consisted just in this: that He might, if He pleased, avoid death. It was because Peter's words, "This be far from Thee," touched a deep chord in His own spirit, and strengthened that within Himself which made Him tremble and wish that

God's will could in any other wise be accomplished—it was this which caused Him so sharply and suddenly to rebuke Peter. Peter's words penetrated to what was lurking near at hand as His normal temptation. We may very readily underrate the trial and temptation of Christ, and thus have only a formal, not a real, esteem for His manhood. We always underrate it when we do not fully apprehend His human nature, and believe that He was tempted in all points as we are. But, on the other hand, we underrate it if we forget that His position was wholly different from ours. That Jesus had abundant nerve and courage no reader of the Gospels can, of course, doubt. He was calm in the midst of a storm which terrified experienced boatmen; in riots that threatened

His life, in the hands of soldiers striving to torment Him and break Him down, in the presence of judges and enemies, He maintained a dignity which only the highest courage could maintain. That such a Person should have quailed at the prospect of physical suffering, which thousands of men and women have voluntarily and calmly faced, is simply impossible to believe. Neither was it entirely His perception of the spiritual significance of death which made it to Him a far more painful prospect than to any other. Certainly this clear perception of the meaning of death did add immensely to its terrors; but if we are even to begin to understand His trial—and begin is all we can do—we must bear in mind what Peter had just confessed, and what Jesus Himself knew—that He was the

Christ. It was this which made the difference. Socrates could toss off the poison as unmoved as if it had been a sleeping-draught, because he was dying for himself alone. Jesus could only with trembling take into His hand the fatal cup, because He knew that He was standing for all men. If He failed, all failed. Everything hung upon Him. The general who spends the whole night pacing his tent, debating the chances of battle on the morrow, is not tormented with the thought of his own private fate, but with the possibilities of disaster to his men and to his country, if his design or his skill should at any moment of the battle fail. Jesus was human; and we deny His humanity, and fail to give Him the honour due to it, if we do not recognise the difficulty which He must always have felt in believing that His single act could save the world, and the burden of responsibility which must have weighed upon Him when He realised that it was by the Spirit He maintained in life and in death, that God meant to bless all men. It was because He knew Himself to be the Christ, and because every man depended upon Him as the Christ, and because, therefore, the whole blessing God meant for the world depended upon His maintaining faith in God through the most trying circumstances—it was because of this that He trembled lest all should end in failure. It was this which drove Him again, and again, and again to the hills to spend all night in prayer, in laying His burden upon the only Strength that could bear it.

But in retiring in order, with

deliberation, finally to dedicate Himself to death, this temptation must of necessity appear in all its strength. It is only in presence of all that can induce Him to another course that He can resolve upon the God-appointed way. As He prays two figures necessarily rise before Him, and intensify the temptation. Moses and Elias were God's greatest servants in the past, and neither of them had passed to glory through so severe an ordeal. Moses, with eye undimmed and strength unabated, was taken from earth by a departure so easy that it was said to be "by the kiss of God." Elijah, instead of removal by death, ascended to his rest in a chariot of fire. Was it not possible that as easy an exodus might befit Him? Might not this ignominious death He looked forward to make it impossible for the people to believe in Him? How could they rank Him with those old prophets whom God had dealt with so differently and so plainly honoured? Would people not almost necessarily accept the death of the cross as proof that He was abandoned? Nay, did not their sacred books justify them in considering Him accursed of God? Was He correct in His interpretation of the Scriptures—an interpretation which led Him to believe that the Messiah must suffer and die, but which none of His friends admitted, and none of the authorities and skilled interpreters in His country admitted? Was it not, after all, possible that His kingdom might be established by other means? We can see but a small part of the force of these temptations, but if the presence of those august figures intensified the normal temptation of this period, their presence was also a very effectual aid against this temptation. In their presence His anticipated end could no longer be called death; rather the departure, or, as the narrative says, the Exodus. The eternal will and mighty hand which had guided and upheld Moses when he bore the responsibility and toil of emancipating a host of slaves from the most powerful of rulers would uphold Jesus in the infinitely weightier responsibilities which now lay upon Him. Elijah, also, at a crisis of his people's history, had stood alone against all the might and malignity of Jezebel and the priests of Baal; alone, and with death staring him in the face, he confessed God, and, by his single-handed victory, wrought deliverance for the whole people.

Their combined voice, therefore, says to Jesus, "Banish all fear; look forward to your decease at Jerusalem as about to effect an immeasurably grander deliverance than that which gave freedom to your people. Do not shrink from trusting that the sacrifice of One can open up a source of blessing to all. Steadfast submission to God's will is ever the path to glory."

But not only must our Lord have been encouraged and heartened by recalling the individual experiences of these men, but their presence reminds Him of His relation to them in God's purposes; for Moses and Elijah represent the whole Old Testament Church. By the Law and the Prophets had God up to this time dealt with men; through these He had revealed Himself. But Jesus had long since recognised that neither Moses nor Elias, neither Law nor Prophets, were sufficient. The Christ must come to effect a real mediation between God and man; and Jesus knew that He Himself was the Christ. On Him lay the task of making the salvation of the Jews the salvation of the whole world; of bringing all men to Jehovah. It was under pressure of this responsibility that He had searched the Scriptures, and found in the Scriptures what those had not found—that it was necessary that Christ should suffer and so enter into glory.

Probably it was not so much any one passage of Scripture which had carried home to the mind of Jesus that the Christ must die. We may seek for that in vain; it was His perception of the real needs of men, and of what the

Law and the Prophets had done to satisfy these needs, that showed Him what remained for the final Revealer and Mediator to accomplish. The Law and the Prophets had told men that God is holy, and that men's blessedness, even as God's blessedness, lies in holiness. But this very teaching seemed to widen the breach between men and God, and to make union between them truly hopeless. By the law came not union with God, but the knowledge of sin. To put it shortly, fellowship or union with God, which is the beginning and end of all religion, is but another name for holiness. Holiness is union with God, and holiness can better be secured by revealing the holy God as a God of love than by law or by prophets. It is this holy love and loving holiness that the cross of Christ brings home to every heart. This revelation of the Father, no document and no officials could possibly make; only the Beloved Son, only one who stood in a personal relation to the Father, and was of the same nature, as truly divine as human. Therefore the voice goes forth annulling all previous utterances, and turning all eyes to Jesus— "Hear Him!" Therefore, as often as the mind of Christ was employed on this subject, so often did He see the necessity of death. It was only by dying that men's sins could be expiated, and only by dying the fulness of God's love could be exhibited. The Law and the Prophets spoke to Him always, and now once more of the decease He must accomplish at Jerusalem. They spoke of His death, because it was His death that was presupposed by every sacrifice of the Law;

by every prophecy that foretold good to man. The Law found its highest fulfilment in the most lawless of transgressions; prophecy found its richest in that which seemed to crush out hope itself.

Nothing, then, could have been more opportune than this for the encouragement of our Lord. On earth He had found incredulity among His best friends; incapacity to see why He should die; indifference to His object here. He now meets with those who, with breathless interest, await His death as if it were the one only future event. In their persons He sees, at one view, all who had put their trust in God from the foundation of the world; all who had put faith in a sacrifice for sin, knowing it was God's appointment, and that He would vindicate His own wisdom and truth by finding a real propitiation; all who, through dark and troublous times, had strained to see the consolation of Israel; all who, in the misery of their own thought, had still believed that there was a true glory for men somewhere to be attained; all who through the darkness and storm and fear of earth had trusted in God, scarcely daring to think what would become of their trust, but assured that God had spoken, nay, had covenanted with His people, and finding true rest in Him. When all these now stand before our Lord in the persons of Moses and Elias, the hitherto mediators between God and man, must not their waiting eyes, their longing, trustful expectation, have confirmed His resolve that their hope should not be put to shame? The whole anxiety of guilty con-

THE TRANSFIGURATION. 59

sciences, the whole hope of men awakened, the whole longing sigh for a God revealed, that had breathed from the ancient Church, at once became audible to His ear. At once He felt the dependence of all who had died in faith in the promise. He meets the eager, questioning gaze of all who had hoped for salvation concentrated on Himself. Is this He who can save the lost, He who can bear the weight of a world's dependence? What an appeal there is here to His compassion! How steadfastly now does He set His face towards Jerusalem, feeling straitened till the world's salvation is secured, and all possibility of failure for ever at an end.

This, then, was for Jesus an appeal that was irresistible. As the full meaning of all that God had done for His people through Law and Prophets was borne in upon Him, He saw that He must die. Now, for the last time, He put aside all His hesitations, and as He prays, He yields Himself to the will of the Father. Those are the supreme moments in human life when man, through sore conflict and at great cost, gives himself up to the will of God. Never was there so sore a conflict, and never so much joy as here. His face was transfigured; it beamed with the light and peace of heaven that shone from within. The eyes of the disciples closed on a face, every line of which they knew and loved—a face full of wisdom and resolve and deep-founded peace, showing marks of trouble, of trial, of endurance, of premature age; their eyes opened upon a face that shines with a preternatural radiance—a face expressing, more

than ever face had done, the
dignity and glory and joy of perfect harmony with God. He was
God-possessed, and the Divine
glory shone from His face. It was
at the moment of His yielding all
to God that Jesus attained His
highest glory. Man's life is transformed when he allows God's will
to fill it and shine through it; his
person is transformed when he
divests himself of self-will, and
allows God wholly to possess it.

How easy was it for the disciples
at that hour to hear Him; to listen
now when He spoke of the cross,
which, for Him and for all His
disciples, is the path leading from
earth to heaven, from what is
selfishly human to true human
glory! It is on the cross that
Jesus is truly enthroned. It is
because He became the Servant of
all that He is greatest of all. If

any one could rival Him in the service he would rival Him in the glory. It is because He gave Himself for us, willing to do all to save us in our direst need, that He takes a place in our confidence and in our heart that belongs to no other. He becomes the one absolute need of every man, because He is that which brings us to God, and gives God to us.

Hear Him, therefore, when, through His Providence, He preaches to you this difficult lesson. If your difficulties and distresses are real; if you cannot labour without thinking of them; if you cannot rest from labour through fear of their possessing you; if your troubles have assumed so hard a form, so real a place in your life, that all else has come to seem unreal and empty, then remember that He whose end was to be eternal glory chose sorrow, that He might break a way to glory through human suffering. If there is nothing in your lot in life which crosses and humbles you; if there is nothing in your circumstances which compels you to see that this life is not for self-indulgence and self-gratification, then still you must win participation in your Lord's glory by accepting His lowliness and heavenliness of mind. It is not to outward success that you are called in His kingdom, it is to inward victory. You are called to meekness, and lowliness, and mercy; to the losing of your life in this world, that you may have life everlasting.

Notice, in conclusion, the impression made on the disciples, as disclosed in Peter's words, "It is good to be here." Peter knew when he was in good company. He was not very wise himself, but he had sense enough to recognise wisdom in others. He was not himself a finished saint, but he had a hearty appreciation of those who had attained saintliness. He had reverence, power to recognise, and ungrudgingly to worship, what was good. He had an honest delight in seeing his Master honoured, a delight which, perhaps, some of us envy. It was not a forced expression, it was not a feigned delight. He was a man who always felt that something should be said, and so here what was uppermost came out. Why did Peter feel it was good for him to be there? Possibly it was in part because here was glory without shame; recognition and homage without suffering; but no doubt partly because he felt that in such company he was a better man than elsewhere. Christ kept him right; seemed to understand him better than others; to consider him more. There was no resentment on Peter's part on account of the severe answers he received from Christ. He knew these were just, and he had learned to trust his Lord; and it suddenly flashes upon him that, if only he could live quietly with Jesus in such retirement as they then enjoyed, he would be a better man. We have the same consciousness as Peter, that if ever we are right-minded and disposed for good, and able to make sacrifices and become a little heavenly; if ever we hate sin cordially—it is when we are in the presence of Christ. If we find it as impossible as Peter did to live retired from all conflict and intercourse with all kinds of men; if, like Peter, we have to descend into a valley ringing with demoniacs' cries; if we are called upon to deal with the world as it actually is—deformed, dehumanised by sin; is it nothing that we can assure ourselves of the society and friendship of One who means to remove all suffering and all sin, and who does so, not by a violent act of authority, but by sympathy and patient love, so that we can be His proper instruments, and in healing and helping others, help and heal ourselves!

Indiscreet Importunity.

INDISCREET IMPORTUNITY.

"I gave thee a king in mine anger."
HOSEA xiii. 11.
"Ye know not what ye ask."
MATTHEW xx. 22.
PSALM lxxviii. 27-31.

THAT God sometimes suffers men to destroy themselves, giving them their own way, although He knows it is ruinous, and even putting into their hands the scorpion they have mistaken for a fish, is an indubitable and alarming fact. Perhaps no form of ruin covers a man with such shame or sinks him to such hopelessness as when he finds that what he has persistently clamoured for and refused to be content without, has proved the bitterest and most disastrous element in his life. This particular form of ruin is nowhere described with more careful and significant detail than in the narrative of Israel's determination to have a king over them like other nations. Samuel, forseeing the evils which would result from their choice, remonstrated with them and reminded them of their past success, and pointed out the advantageous elements in their present condition. But there is a point at which desire becomes deaf and blind, and the evil of it can be recognised only after it is gratified. God therefore "gave them a king in His anger."

The truth, then, which is embodied in this incident, and which is liable to reappear in the experience of any individual, is this, that sometimes God yields to importunity, and grants to men what

He knows will be no blessing to them. "It is a thing," says South, "partly worth our wonder, partly our compassion, that what the greatest part of men most passionately desire, that they are generally most unfit for; so that at a distance they court that as an enjoyment, which upon experience they find a plague and a great calamity." It is astonishing how many things we desire for the same reason as the Israelites sought a king, merely that we may have what other people have. We may not definitely covet our neighbour's house or his wife or his position or anything that is his; but deep within us remains the scarcely-conscious conviction that we have not all we might and ought to have until our condition more resembles his. We take our ideas of happiness from what we see in other people, and have little originality to devise any special and more appropriate enjoyment or success. Fashion or tradition or the necessity of one class in society has promoted certain possessions and conditions to the rank of extremely desirable or even necessary elements of happiness, and forthwith we desire them, without duly considering our own individuality and what it is that must always constitute happiness for us, or what it is that fits us for present usefulness. Health, position, fame, a certain settlement in life, income, marriage; such things are eagerly sought by thousands, and they are sought without sufficient discrimination, or at any rate without a well-informed weighing of consequences. We refuse, too, to see that already without those things our condition has much advantage, and that we are actually happy. We may be dimly conscious that our tastes are not precisely those of other men, and that if the ordinary ways of society are the best men can devise for spending life satisfactorily, these are scarcely the ways that will suit us. Yet, like petted children, we continue persistently to cry for the thing we have not. Sometimes it is a mere question of waiting. The thing we sigh for will come in time, but not yet. To wait is the test of many persons; and if they are impatient, they fail in the one point that determines the whole. Many young persons seem to think life will all be gone before they taste any of its sweets. They must have everything at once, and cannot postpone any of its enjoyments or advantages. No quality is more fatal to success and lasting happiness than impatience.

This being a common attitude of mind towards fancied blessings, how does God deal with it? For a long time He may in compassion withhold the fatal gift. He may in pity disregard our petulant clamour. And He may in many ways bring home to our minds that the thing we crave is in several respects unsuitable. We may become conscious under His discipline that without it we are less entangled with the world and with temptation; that we can live more holily and more freely as we are, and that to quench the desire we have would be to choose the better part. God may make it plain to us that it is childish to look upon this one thing as the supreme and only good. Providential obstacles are thrown in our way, difficulties amounting almost to impossibilities absolutely prevent us for a while from attaining our object, and give us time to collect ourselves and take thought. And not only are we prevented from attaining this one object, but in other respects our life is enriched and gladdened, so that we might be expected to be content. If we cannot have a king like other nations, we have the best of Judges in abundance. And experience of this kind will convince the subject of it that a Providence shapes our ends, even although the lesson it teaches may remain unlearnt.

For man's will is never forced: and therefore if we continue to pin our happiness to this one object, and refuse to find satisfaction and fruit in life without it, God "gives in anger" what we have resolved to obtain. He gives it in its bare earthly form, so that as soon as we receive it our soul sinks in shame. Instead of expanding our nature and bringing us into a finished and satisfactory condition, and setting our life in right relations with other men, we find the new gift to be a curse to us, hampering us, cutting us off in unexpected ways from our usefulness, thwarting and blighting our life round its whole circumference.

For a man is never very long in discovering the mischief he has done by setting his own wisdom above God's, by underrating God's goodness and overriding God's will. When Samuel remonstrated with Israel and warned them that their king would tyrannise over them, all the answer he got was: "Nay, but we will have a king to rule over us." But, not many days after, they came to Samuel with a very different petition: "Pray for thy servants unto the Lord thy God, that we die not; for we have added unto all our sins this evil, to ask us a king." So it is always; we speedily recognise the difference between God's wisdom and our own. What seemed neglect on His part is now seen to be care, and what we murmured at as niggardliness and needless harshness we now admire as tenderness. Those at least are our second and wiser thoughts, even although at first we may be tempted with Manoah when he saw his son blind and fettered in the Philistine dungeon, to exclaim,

> What thing good
> Pray'd for, but often proves our woe, our bane?
> I prayed for children and thought barrenness

In wedlock a reproach; I gain'd a son
And such a son as all men hail'd me
 happy.
Who would be now a father in my stead?
Oh, wherefore did God grant me my
 request,
And as a blessing with such pomp
 adorn'd?
Why are His gifts desirable, to tempt
Our earnest prayers, then giv'n with
 solemn hand
As graces, draw a scorpion's tail behind?

Such, I say, may be our first thoughts; but when the first bitterness and bewilderment of disappointment are over, when reason and right feeling begin to dominate, we own that the whole history of our prayer and its answer has been most humiliating to us, indeed, but most honouring to God. We see as never before how accurately our character has been understood, how patiently our evil propensities have been resisted,

how truly our life has been guided
towards the highest ends.

The obvious lessons are:—

1. Be discreet in your importunity. Two parables are devoted to the inculcation of importunity. And it is a duty to which our own intolerable cravings drive us. But there is an importunity which offends God. There is a spiritual instinct which warns us when we are transgressing the bounds of propriety; a perception whereby Paul discerned, when he had prayed thrice for the removal of the thorn in his flesh, that it would not be removed. There are things about which a heavenly-minded person feels it to be unbecoming to be over-solicitous; and there are things regarding which it is somehow borne in upon us that we are not to attain them. There are natural disabilities, physical or

mental or social weaknesses and embarrassments, regarding which we sometimes cannot but cry out to God for relief, and yet as we cry we feel that they will not be removed, and that we must learn to bear the burden cheerfully.

2. On the other hand, we must not be false in prayer. We must utter to God our real desires in their actual intensity; while at the same time we must learn to moderate desires which we see to be unpleasing to God. We must learn to say with truth:

> Not what we wish but what we want
> Thy favouring grace supply;
> The good unasked, in mercy grant,
> The ill, though asked, deny.

Learn why God does not make the coveted blessing accessible to you, and you will learn to pray freely and wisely. Try to discover whether there is not some peculiar advantage attaching to your present state—some more wholesome example you can furnish, some more helpful attitude towards others; some healthier exercise of the manlier graces of Christianity, which could not be maintained were your request granted.

3. If your life is marred by the gift you have wrung by your importunity from a reluctant God, be wise and humble in your dealing with that gift. If you have suddenly and painfully learned that in the ordinary-looking circumstances of your life God is touching you at every point, and if you clearly see that in giving you the fruit of your desires He is punishing you, there is one only way by which you can advance to a favourable settlement, and that is by a real submission to God. Perhaps

in no circumstances is a man more tempted to break with God. At first he cannot reconcile himself to the idea that ruin should be the result of prayer, and he is inclined to say, If this be the result of waiting on God, the better course is to refuse His guidance. In his heart he knows he is wrong, but there is an appearance of justice in what he says, and it is so painful to have the heart broken, to admit we have been foolish and wrong, and humbly to beseech God to repair the disasters our own self-will has wrought.

Shame on Account of God's Displeasure.

SHAME ON ACCOUNT OF GOD'S DISPLEASURE.

"And the Lord said unto Moses, If her father had but spit in her face, should she not be ashamed seven days? Let her be shut out from the camp seven days, and after that let her be received in again."—NUMBERS xii. 14.

THE incident recorded in this chapter is of a painful character. Petty jealousies discovered themselves in the most distinguished family of Israel. Through the robes of the anointed and sacred High Priest the throbbings of a heart stirred with evil passion were discernible. Aaron and Miriam could not bear that even their own brother should occupy a position of exceptional dignity, and with ignorant pretentiousness aspired to equality with him. It is to the punishment of this sin that our attention is here called. This punishment fell directly on Miriam, possibly because the person of the High Priest was sacred, and had he been incapacitated all Israel would have suffered in their representative; possibly because the sin, as it shows traces of a peculiarly feminine jealousy, was primarily the sin of Miriam; and partly because, in her punishment, Aaron suffered a sympathetic shame, as is apparent from his impassioned appeal to Moses in her behalf.

The noteworthy feature of the incident and its most impressive lesson are found in the fact that, although the healing and forgiveness sought for Miriam were not refused, God is represented as resenting the speedy oblivion of the offence on account of which the leprosy had been sent and of the Divine displeasure incurred. There was cause to apprehend that the whole matter might be too quickly wiped out and forgotten, and that the sinners, reinstated in their old positions, should think too lightly of their offence. This detrimental suddenness God takes measures to prevent. Had an earthly father manifested his displeasure as emphatically as God had now shown His, Miriam could not for a time have held up her head. God desires that the shame which results from a sense of His displeasure should last at least as long. He therefore enjoins something like a penance; He removes His stroke, but provides for the moral effects of it being sufficiently impressed on the spirit to be permanent.

Three points are involved in the words:

1. Our keener sense of man's displeasure than of God's.

2. The consequent possibility of accepting pardon with too light a heart.

3. The means of preventing such acceptance of pardon.

1. *We are much more sensitive to the displeasure of man than to that of God.* Men have several methods of expressing their opinion of us and their feeling toward us; and these methods are quite effectual for their purpose. There is an instinctive and exact correspondence between our feelings and every slightest hint of disapprobation on the part of our acquaintances; and so readily and completely does the mere carriage of any person convey to us his estimate of our conduct that explicit denunciation is seldom required. The mode of expressing opinion

which is cited in the text is the most forcible Eastern mode of expressing contempt. When one man spits in the face of another, no one, and least of all the suffering party, can have the slightest doubt of the esteem in which the one holds the other. If an insolent enemy were to spit in the face of a slain foe, the dead man might almost be expected to blush or to rise and avenge the insult. But comparing His methods with such a method as this, God awards the palm to His own for explicitness and emphasis. He speaks of the most emphatic and unambiguous of human methods with a "but," as if it could scarcely be compared with His expressions of displeasure. "If her father had *but* spit in her face"—if that were all—but something immensely more expressive than that has happened to her.

God, therefore, would have us ponder the punishments of sin, and find in them the emphatic expressions of His judgment of our conduct and of ourselves. He resents our shamelessness, and desires that we consider His judgments till our callousness is removed. The case stands thus: God is long-suffering, slow to anger, not of a fault-finding, ever-chiding nature, but most loving and most just; and this God has recorded against us the strongest possible condemnation. This God, who cannot do what is not most just, and who cannot make mistakes, this unfurious and holy God, whose opinion of us represents the very truth, has pronounced us to be wicked and worthless; and we seem scarcely at all impressed by the declaration. God's judgment of us is not only absolutely true, but it must also take effect; so that what He has pronounced against us will be seen written in the facts bearing upon and entering into our life. But, although we know this, we are for the most part as unmoved as if in hearing God's judgment pronounced against us we had heard but the sighing of the wind or any other inarticulate, unintelligible sound. There is a climax of ignominy in having excited in the Divine mind feelings of displeasure against us. One might suppose a man would die of shame, and could not bear to live conscious of having merited the condemnation and punishment of such a Being; one might suppose that the breath of God's disapproval would blast every blessing to us, and that so long as we know ourselves displeasing to Him His sweetest gifts must be bitter to us; but the coldness of a friend gives us more thought, and the contempt of men as contemptible as ourselves affects us with a more genuine confusion.

God's demand, then, is reasonable. He would have us feel before Him as much shame as we feel before men, the same kind of shame—shame with the same blush and burning in it, not shame of any sublimated, fictitious kind. He desires us individually to take thought, and to say to ourselves: "Suppose a man had proved against me even a small part of what is proved against me by God: suppose some wise, just, and honourable man had said of me and believed such things as God has said: suppose he had said, and said truly, that I had robbed him, betrayed trust, and was unworthy of his friendship, would the shame be no more poignant than that which I feel when God denounces me?" How trifling are the causes which make us blush before our fellows: a little awkwardness, the slightest accident which makes us appear blundering, some scarcely perceptible incongruity of dress, an infinitesimal error in manner or in accent—anything is enough to make us uneasy in the company of those we esteem. It is God's reasonable demand that for those gross iniquities and bold transgressions of which we are conscious we should manifest some heartfelt shame—a shame that does not wholly lack the poignancy and agitation of the confusion we feel in presence of human judgment.

2. *The consequent possibility of accepting the pardon of sin with too*

light a heart. To ask for pardon without real shame is to treat sin lightly; and to treat sin lightly is to treat God lightly. Nothing more effectually deadens the moral sense than the habit of asking pardon without a due sense of the evil of sin. We ask God to forgive us our debts, and we do so in so inconsiderate a spirit that we go straightway and contract heavier debts. The friend who repays the ten pounds we had lent him and asks for a new loan of twenty, does not commend himself to our approval. He is no better who accepts pardon as if it cost God nothing.

3. *The means of preventing a too light-hearted acceptance of pardon.* Under the ceremonial prescriptions enjoined on Miriam lay some moral efficacy. A person left for a full week without the camp must, in

separation from accustomed companionship, intercourse, and occupations, have been thrown upon his or her own thoughts. No doubt it is often while engaged in our ordinary occupations that the strongest light is flashed upon our true spiritual condition. It is while in the company of other people that we catch hints which seem to interpret to us our past and reveal to us our present state. But these glimpses and hints often pass without result, because we do not find leisure to follow them up. There must be some kind of separation from the camp if we are to know ourselves, some leisure gained for quiet reflection. It is due to God that we be at some pains to ascertain with precision our actual relation to His will.

The very feeling of being outcast, unworthy to mingle with

former associates and friends, must have been humbling and instructive. Miriam had been the foremost woman in Israel; now she would gladly have changed places with the least known and be lost among the throng from the eye of wonder, pity, contempt or cruel triumph. All sin makes us unworthy of fellowship with the people of God. And the feeling that we are thus unworthy, instead of being lightly and callously dismissed, should be allowed to penetrate and stir the conscience.

If the leprosy departed from Miriam as soon as Moses prayed, yet the shock to her physical system, and the revulsion of feeling consequent on being afflicted with so loathsome a disease, would tell upon her throughout the week. All consequences of sin, which are prolonged after pardon, have their proper effect and use in begetting shame. We are not to evade what conscience tells us of the connection between our sin and many of the difficulties of our life. We are not to turn away from this as a morbid view of providence; still less are we to turn away because in this light sin seems so real and so hideous. Miriam must have thought, "If this disgusting condition of my body, this lassitude and nervous trembling, this fear and shame to face my fellows, be the just consequence of my envy and pride, how abominable must these sins be." And we are summoned to similar thoughts. If this pursuing evil, this heavy clog that drags me down, this insuperable difficulty, this disease, or this spiritual and moral weakness be the fair natural consequence of my sin, if these things are in the natural world what my sin is in the spiritual, then my sin must be a much greater evil than I was taking it to be.

But especially are we rebuked for all light-heartedness in our estimate of sin by remembering Him who went without the camp bearing our reproach. It is when we see Christ rejected of men, and outcast for us and for our sin, that we feel true shame. To find one who so loves me and enters into my position that He feels more keenly than myself the shame I have incurred; to find one who so understands God's holiness and is Himself so pure that my sin affects Him with the profoundest shame —this is what pierces my heart with an altogether new compunction, with an arrow that cannot be shaken out. And this connection of Christ with our sin is actual.

If Paul felt himself so bound up with his fellow-Christians that he blushed for them when they erred, and could say with truth, "Who is weak and I am not weak, who is offended and I turn not?" much more truly may Christ say, Who sins and I am not ashamed? And if He thus enters into a living sympathy with us, shall not we enter into sympathy with Him, and go without the camp bearing His reproach, which, indeed, is ours; striving, though it cost us much shame and self-denial, to enter heartily into His feelings at our sins, and not letting our union to Him be a mere name or an inoperative tie which effects no real assimilation in spirit between us and Him.

Naaman Cured.

NAAMAN CURED.

There is no Scripture story better known than that of Naaman, the Syrian. It is memorable not only because artistically told, but because it is so full of human feeling and rapid incident, and so fertile in significant ideas. The little maid, whose touch set in motion this drama, is an instance of the adaptability of the Jew. Nothing seemed less likely than that this captive girl should carry with her into Syria anything of much value to any one. Possessions she had none. Friends she might have, only if she could make them. As a captive in a foreign land she might reasonably have put aside all hope of obtaining any influence, and might naturally have sought only to benefit herself. But she was a girl with a heart. She at once took an interest in her new home, and saw with sorrowful surprise that wealth could not purchase immunity from participation in the ordinary human distresses, nor guarded gates forbid disease to pass in. Brooding from day to day over the stories she had heard of Elisha's power, and listening to her mistress's account of the failure of still another attempted cure, she exclaims with childlike confidence and earnestness, "Would God my lord were with the prophet that is in Samaria! then would he recover him of his leprosy." And thus her natural interest in the troubles of other people, her cheerful and spirited acceptance of her position, and the sense that taught her to make the most of it, brought her this great opportunity of doing an important service. No one can lay the blame of his uselessness and lack of good influence on his lack of opportunity, if he is in contact with men at all, for wherever there are human beings there are sorrows to be sympathised with, wants to be relieved, characters to be fashioned.

And while this Jewish maid was utilising her captivity, her parents, if alive, would be eating their hearts out with anxiety and anguish, imagining for their daughter the worst of destinies. Instead of the horrors which usually follow such a captivity, she is cared for in a comfortable home. Little did the parents think that there was any work to be done in Syria, which none could so well do as their little girl. The Lord had need of her, and knew that when the parents heard all they would not resent that their daughter had been thus employed. None of us see much further into the ways of Providence than those parents saw. Now, as then, those who are bound up in one another are separated, in order that ends even more important than the growth and gratification of natural affections may be attained.

Significant, also, is the dismay of Joram, King of Israel, when he received the letter bidding him find healing for Naaman. So little did he believe in Elisha's power that he concluded the King of Syria sought to pick a quarrel with him by asking him for a favour he knew he could not grant. But while the king is helplessly tearing his clothes in a passion of despair, Elisha sends him a message which, at least for the present, gives him some calmness: "Why hast thou rent thy clothes? Let him come now to me, and he shall know that there is a prophet in Israel." Elisha is ashamed that the King of Israel should have exhibited such weakness before a foreign potentate. He feels that the honour of Israel's God is implicated, and boldly takes upon himself the responsibility of the cure. Bold it certainly was, and tells of a confident faith that God will be faithful to His servants. The king had no such faith. There was a power resident in Israel of which he took no account. Like many other governments, this Israelitish monarchy was unaware of its own resources, because it did not condescend to reckon what was spiritual. Frequently in civil history you find governments brought face to face with matters for which they are, with all their resources, incompetent. In modern Europe, and as much in our own country as in others, everything gives place to politics. Nothing stirs so much excitement. Differences in religion do not sever men as differences in politics do. We should, therefore, recognise what is here suggested, and should counterbalance an undue regard for political movements and political power by the remembrance that the hardest tasks of all are accomplished by quite another power, and by a power which the politician often overlooks. What have we seen time after time in our own Parliament, but the civil power rending its garments over evils which it cannot cure? Are not the remedies which have been proposed for prevalent vices absurdly incompetent? And it is the Church's shame if she cannot step forward and confidently say, You cannot deal with such things; hand them over to me. There must always be "distempers of society" which rot the very life out of a nation, and for which legislation and criminal law are wholly inadequate. Honest-minded men who will not trifle with alarming abuses, who will not pretend they have found a remedy, must simply rend their garments in their presence. And it is well that in our day, as in others, there are men who, trusting in personal effort and Divine aid, practically say to Government, "Leave these things to us." Christian charity and practical wisdom have, in our day, effected a good deal more than the healing of one leprous grandee, even if as yet the spiritual force that resides in the community is only spasmodically and partially applied to existing evil.

Elisha's treatment of Naaman was intended to bring him into direct and conscious dependence on God; or, in other words, to produce humility and faith. Some persons are crushed and mastered by pain and sickness, and some gain in spiritual worth what they lose in physical strength. But Naaman's disease had as yet done little to instruct him. He came as a great man, with his servants, and chariots, and piles of money, to purchase a cure from a skilled man. He did not see what Elisha plainly saw, that if this blessing came at all, it must come from Israel's

God, and that with Jehovah no man could barter or be on bargaining terms, but must accept freely what was freely given. Therefore Elisha refuses even to see him, that Naaman might understand it was with God he had to do; and by refusing a single penny of payment he compelled the Syrian to humble himself and accept his cure as a gift.

And probably the incident finds a place in the sacred history because it marked an important step in the knowledge of God. It was an early instance of the conquests which the God of Israel was to make among the heathen, a distinct and legible proof that whoever from among the outlying nations appealed to Him for help would receive the blessing he sought. But it was more than this, it emphasized the freeness of all

God's gifts. Nothing could be purchased from Jehovah; everything must be received as a gift. This was a new idea to the heathen, and probably to many of the Israelites also. Certainly it is an idea that is only dimly apprehended by ourselves. Our dealing with one another is to so large an extent governed by the idea that nothing can be had for nothing, that we carry this idea into our dealings with God, and expect only what we can earn and claim. It is a wholesome pride that prompts us to work at anything rather than be dependent on other men, but it is a most unwholesome and ignorant pride that forbids us to acknowledge our dependence on God, and to accept freely what He freely gives. Until we learn to live in God, to own Him as alone having life in Himself, and to accept from Him life and all that sustains it, both physical and spiritual, we are not recognising the truth and living in it. Our good deeds and good feelings, our repentances and righteous intentions and endeavours, are as much out of place as a means of procuring God's favour and help as Naaman's talents of silver and pieces of gold. We have God's favour irrespective of our merit, and we must humble ourselves to accept it as His free gift, which we could not earn and have not earned.

Naaman no sooner saw that Jehovah was a living and true God than he perceived that certain practical difficulties would result from this belief. Sometimes men do not connect their belief with their practice; they do not let their left hand know what their right hand is doing. But Naaman foresaw that, as hitherto, he would still be expected to enter the temple of the god Rimmon when his master went to worship. And he wished Elisha's authority for this measure of conformity.

In our own country men have been severely tested by acts of conformity. And nothing gives the conscience of the whole people so decided a lift as when men prefer disgrace or death to a conformity which they believe to be wrong.

Had Naaman been as uncompromising as Daniel, who would not conform even so far as to pray in a different corner of his room, or as the Christian soldiers who suffered death rather than throw a pinch of incense on the altar before the Emperor's image, possibly Elisha would have given him greater commendation than the mere acquiescence pronounced in the words, "Go in peace."

But in exculpation of Naaman it is to be said that he did not hide his new conviction, but built an altar to Jehovah in Damascus. And especially it is to be remarked that in his case these acts of conformity were not proposed as a test of his adherence to the religion of the country; and this makes all the difference. Had Naaman's master commanded him to bow in the house of Rimmon as a test of his acknowledgment of the Syrian god, Naaman would have refused; but so long as it was a mere act or courtesy to his master, the formal act of a courtier, from which no inferences could be drawn, he might reasonably continue it. To receive the communion kneeling is customary in some churches, and so long as one is allowed to put his own interpretation on the attitude, no harm can come of it. But at one time this attitude was the test by which two great and antagonistic parties in England were distinguished from one another; a meaning was put upon the act which made it impossible to every man who could not accept that meaning. Conformity then was sin, unless conviction went with the outward act. In many points of conduct this is a distinction of importance. There are many things which we may do so far as the thing itself is concerned, but which we may not do when the public mind is agitated upon that point and will draw certain inferences from our conduct. There are many things which to us have no moral significance at all, any more than sitting at one side or other of our table; but if a moral significance is attached to such things by other people, and if they invite us to do them or to leave them undone as a test of our attitude towards God or Christianity or of our moral bent, then we must beware of misleading other people and defiling our own conscience. Bowing in the house of Rimmon meant nothing new to Naaman; it was not worship; it was no more than turning round a street corner when the king had hold of his arm. To him the idol was now, as to Paul, "nothing in the world." But if the king had said, " You must bow to show the people that you worship Syria's god," then plainly the bowing would have been unjustifiable. And similarly, if a matter which to us is of no moral significance becomes a test of our disposition or attitude towards truth, we must be guided in our conduct not solely by our own view of the indifference of the matter, but also by the significance attached to it by other people. There are other points of conduct regarding which we have no need to consult any prophet; points in which we are asked to conform to a custom we know to be bad, or to follow and countenance other men in what we know to be unwholesome for us. To conform in such cases is to train ourselves in hypocrisy; it is to say Lord, Lord, while we allow the world actually to rule our life.

The Lame Man at the Temple Gate.

THE LAME MAN AT THE TEMPLE GATE.

Acts iii. 1-8.

Although this miracle was followed by consequences so serious as to make it a landmark in the history of those early days of the Church, it was not itself the result of deliberation or contrivance. Peter and John were, as usual, on their way to evening prayer in the Temple. These two men had much to gain from one another, and they kept much together. In study, in business, in Christian work, in life generally every one is the better of the friend who supplements his own character. Happy he whose closest friend of all provokes only to love and good works, and calls out only what is best in him. It is, if not essential to the growth and health of the spiritual life, most desirable to have a friend with whom intercourse is absolutely free and frank; one to whom it is the natural thing to explain the actual state of the spirit, and utter our most sceptical or our most devout thoughts, and who can be trusted to respond charitably, confidentially, and wisely to all communications. The Church owes much to the friendship of Peter and John, as well as to each individually.

On how small a contingency did this miracle hinge. Had Peter happened to have had a penny he would have dropped it in the beggar's palm and passed on, leaving him content with the alms and unconscious of all he had missed. And it is sometimes well for us, as for Peter, that we are baulked in our first intentions towards our friends and our first attempts at being of use. It is well, for example, that we cannot at once rescue every one out of sickness and poverty, for thereby our love is compelled to a deeper consideration and to a thousand kindnesses which find their way to the heart and leave for ever a treasure of happy memory. Our inability to gratify the obvious and clamant want of our friend keeps our thought hovering around him until, at last, we discern how we can confer a better and more enduring, because a more difficult and thoughtful, gift.

Probably Peter had often passed this lame man before. To-day the two Apostles have not together as much as the poor widow with her two mites, and they are passing and thinking as little as we sometimes think of leaving the needy to the charity of others, when suddenly it occurs to Peter that, after all, he has what may be of more service to the beggar than silver or gold. "What I have, that give I thee." The best help we can give is not that which we can give with the hand, and which is current coin, which any one else may give, and which is of the same value, whoever gives it; but rather that which we communicate from our own heart and soul, and which is our own peculiar treasure —the accumulation of a life's experience. To add a little to any one's outward comfort is always worth doing; but to impart to another what becomes life and strength and encouragement perennially within himself is surely better. Frequently the help we chiefly need is nothing outward and material, but that which one bare human spirit can render to another. But, alas! when thrown back upon our inward resources, we are so conscious of our poverty that we think sixpence or a shilling is probably of greater value than anything which can come straight from our spirit.

Of the lame man little is told us which may give us a clue to his state of mind. He was one of those who had been left unhealed by Christ. Often must Christ have passed him, and yet He had never spoken nor laid healing hand upon him. Perhaps during the long hours the lame man sometimes thought of this, and bewailed his own negligence in not using opportunities now for ever gone. He could only look with envy and self-reproach on those who had once been blind, or, like himself, lame, and whom he now saw in perfect health. His feelings were akin to the remorse of those who imagine that their day of grace is gone, and exclaim:

> Thy saints are comforted, I know,
> And love Thy house of prayer;
> I therefore go where others go,
> But find no comfort there.

There is no despair worth calling despair but despair of salvation. But what Christ has not done, an Apostle may do. The lesser instrument may effect what the more powerful has not effected. A feebler ministry may in some cases produce results which the abler ministry has not produced.

Another feature of the beggar's state of mind appears in the listless, mechanical way in which he asks an alms. He had not even troubled to look up. Too commonly human prayer is the monotonous whine of the beggar that scarcely troubles to consider to whom the petition is addressed. Had this man taken the trouble to scan the appearance of those fishermen he would have seen that silver or gold could not be expected. But he had fallen into one chant, uttered as soon as the shadow of the passer-by fell upon him. It is a picture of the unreal and indifferent spirit in which much prayer is offered. There is no harm in asking for certain benefits every day of our life, and no harm in using the same words, if we have chosen these words as the fittest. But there is harm in allowing a form of words to engender monotony and lifelessness in the spirit, so that we never consider carefully the object of our worship and what it is fit that He should give. This cripple had come to be content with the few coppers which would furnish his supper and bed; all the great world with its pleasures, its enterprise, its high places, lay quite beyond his hope; and thus does one find his own soul dying to all that lies beyond daily needs, and forgetful of the great and glorious things that are written of the heirs of God. It is surely a great art to know "who it is that speaks to us, and what is the gift of God."

Peter's first care was to arouse the man. "Look on us!" The man's attention was commanded. All his life he had been training to know faces, to know who would give and who would not give, who would not give if others were looking, and who would give at the gate of the Temple, dropping the coin as into an alms box, without any regard to the want of the beggar. One glance at the frank face of Peter tells him he is about to receive something. That is a man to be trusted. This is a good beginning. Trust in Peter may be the first step to trust in Christ. But many rest at the earliest stage, believing the messenger, but not coming into personal relations with Christ. Many persons wish to be better than they are, and are prepared to do much and sacrifice much in order to attain to a satisfactory spiritual state. What is lacking is personal appeal to Christ. They must recognise, with a conviction wrought in their own mind, that Jesus Christ is the source of spiritual power, and they must, for themselves, appeal directly to Him.

The boldness with which Peter forms or, it might almost be said, forces this personal relation to Christ in the case of this man is surprising. Without a moment's hesitation or inquiry as to whether the man's faith is quickened, Peter cries, "In the name of Jesus Christ of Nazareth, rise up and walk," taking him by the right hand and lifting him up. Peter could not confer health upon the man in spite of his state of mind. If the man had so chosen he might have continued to lie where he was, a cripple. But simultaneously with Peter's faith and authoritative command, the man's own faith was quickened. He believed that in this name, that is, at the command and in the strength of Christ, he could get up; and he arose. It was the contagious confidence of Peter which begat faith in the lame beggar's spirit. And there could not be a more instructive instance of the suddenness with which a human being can be brought into saving relation to Christ. When Peter began his sentence the lame man had no faith, yet he boldly said to him, "In the name of Jesus Christ arise and walk." Men may always thus be summoned to believe on the spot and to act out the commands of Christ.

But in order that such a summons be effectual, two qualities in the apostle are needful. He must not fear failure or rebuff. He must have that humility which seeks the good of others regardless of its own reputation. So long as we fear to expose our own feelings, and to show that we are deeply concerned about the welfare of another person, we shall do little in the way of inspiring faith. Our mouth is kept shut by the fear of fruitlessly exposing our feelings. We are not sure how our advances will be received. We have not the loving humility which braves risks to self.

We must also ourselves have lively faith if we are to communicate faith to others. It was Peter's own faith which carried this man's unbelief by storm. In presence of Peter's confidence he could not but believe. Most men are far more moved by the contagion of others' strong feeling and example than by arguments or verbal appeals. For the diffusion of faith it is a man like Peter that is wanted, who overleaps the obstacles which other men would stop to examine; a man like Luther, erring perhaps in fine points of doctrine, but giving impetus and force to the whole movement in Christ's kingdom, and sweeping along with him a host of weaker and dependent spirits. If we are not propagating faith in Christ, it is mainly because our own faith is meagre and timorous. If we are not producing Christians it is because we are not ourselves in the present experience of His mighty power. And while this is so, our conduct betrays the weakness of our faith, and we chill the kindling warmth in other souls instead of fanning it into flame, and all that proceeds from us is as the frosty wind of an untoward spring-time, that unseasonably marks every springing thing with death.

Possessed of those qualities, any one may communicate that best of all gifts, faith in Christ. The joy of Peter, in discovering that he could impart health and brightness to those who were oppressed by various human ills, is a joy which may be repeated, and was meant to be repeated, in the experience of every Christian. We are not to look hopelessly on the world at large or on our own friends. We are not to think that the pleasure we have in being of substantial service to a friend, we cannot have in the case of that which is most substantial. We are to believe that Christ now has all power in heaven and on earth, and that those who have experienced this power are expected to be the channel of its communication to others. The faith which strengthens and elevates our own spirit may be communicated, upon our effort and prayer, to the heart of others.

www.ingramcontent.com/pod-product-compliance
Lightning Source LLC
Chambersburg PA
CBHW030400170426
43202CB00010B/1436